Be Healed from Within: The reason behind my smile

By: Trineka. Y. Anderson

Acknowledgements

First, I would like to give thanks to God for making it possible for me to use my willpower and determination to write this book. To my grandparents- Davis and Etherine Anderson, my mother Gwenderine Anderson, my sisters- Tiffoni Weathersby and Treyowna Veal: Thank you all for never giving up on me and for helping me to believe in myself. To my late grandfather who always told me to push towards my dreams. He knew I always wanted to be an author so he would encourage me to continue to write. To my nieces and nephews: Thank you for believing in me and helping me to strive harder to reach my goals. To my pastor-the incomparable Pastor Douglas V. Noel and my New Covenant Christian Fellowship Church family: I thank each of you for your love and support. To my best friend that's been there since 9th grade, Lakeisha Smith: I thank you for showing me the true definition of a friend.- To my number one vent buddy Adriana Washington: Thank you for all the late nights you stayed up with me to be my listening ear. To the queens of Team Positive Ministries: Thank you for helping me to find balance. Special thanks to my order of Eastern Star Chapter Esther #34.

Synopsis

Life can sometimes put us in situations where we want to give up. The simple things in life sometimes cause us to struggle. We can sometimes choose money and fame, people, and other things to make life complete other than choosing God and accepting His will for our lives. What happened to totally relying and depending on God? Do not just call Him when you need Him, call Him before you need Him.

Dedication

This book is dedicated to a man who has pushed me beyond my wildest imagination. He was there for me in more ways than one. He always proved to me that I had the ability to achieve and accomplish anything I put my mind and heart to. He said opportunity is just like an open door you have the right to choose. I dedicate this book to my grandfather, Davis Anderson.

It is because of you I made it through some dark and difficult situations. I want to say thank you for always being by my side. Whenever I felt as if I wanted to give up, it was your simple words that helped me to push on. You were always there for me when I needed you most and you always had the right words to say.

You were a man of very few words, but you stood firm to what you believed. You will always be my role model. Thank you for your love and support and for believing in me. I cannot thank you enough for being there to keep me straight and to help me stay focused. On August 5, 2011, my life changed forever. That was the day you told me goodbye on this side of life. It is my prayer that you save a seat for me, and you will forever rest in my heart until we meet again. I love you Grandpa.

Davis "Pomp" Anderson   October 25, 1918- August 5, 2011

Table of Contents

Prologue

Chapter 1- Trusting God Through the Storm

Chapter 2- Understanding God's Plan for You

Chapter 3- Facing Your Fear Through Grace

Chapter 4- Finding Favor with God

Chapter 5- Our Words Have Power

Chapter 6- The Benefits of Prayer

Chapter 7- Seek God with Your Whole Heart

Chapter 8- Run on for God

Chapter 9- How Deep is Your Love for Christ?

Chapter 10- God Is in Control of the Storm

Chapter 11- Have an Attitude of Gratitude

Chapter 12- The Effects of the Secret Place

Chapter 13- Rise Above Your Opposition

Chapter 14- God Will Provide

Chapter 15- Blessings for Praying for Others

Chapter 16- The Importance of Staying in the Game

Prologue

In life, we may plan for one thing to happen, but other things occur. Sometimes we put people, places, and things before God, and this causes us to experience major problems. Heartbreaks, set-ups, setbacks, let-downs, and failures will sometimes make us turn away from God; but it is during these times that we need him most.

Chapter 1

Trusting God Through the Storm

Ever felt like giving up? Have you ever wanted to throw in the towel? Yes, I have been there, but I have learned to trust God through the storm. Although my life has not been easy and I truly had some tough times, God never gave up on me. I have faced several challenges that have enabled me to push a little harder. Trusting God becomes easy when your relationship is stronger.

Building your real relationship with God takes hard work and dedication. Sometimes it may cause you to distance yourself from others. Trusting God when the time comes allows you to know and understand that God is with you and He will not put more on you than you can handle. I have had many situations when I realized that I had to lean and depend on Jesus. Trusting God through the storm takes a whole lot of effort. It helps to build your faith. It also helps you to develop character as you press on to victory.

Character-building and trusting God works hand in hand. One must trust God to become the person He would have you to be. Character-building helps you to grow and understand your God-given purpose in life. Trusting in God starts from within. It is important that we trust God to bring us out of certain situations.

In my past, I have learned to trust God when I felt I had no way out. For example, I have been beating the odds since birth. I was born with a physical disability called cerebral palsy. I had to struggle to stay alive, I was born on June 5, and it was not until December, I was able to finally go home to my family. It took months for me to defeat all the obstacles I faced, such as low birth weight, breathing complications, and later a life-altering disability, but by God's grace, I made it. Another example was when I was about to begin school and I was having mobility issues when it came time to walk. I did not learn to walk until I was about four years of age. My confidence came the day before I began preschool. These instances really taught me to trust God even when it looks like the situation was too hard for me; God intervened in perfect timing. Although I wanted to give up, quit, and throw in the towel, my past obstacles encourage me to push harder.

I love the acronym P.U.S.H.- Pray Until Something Happens. When we are put in situations where we need to trust God, it is very vital that we pray and allow God to do the rest. Trusting in God takes more than lip-service; it takes one's willingness to know how important it is to trust God through the storm. Storms will rise in your life but that is when you must put your faith to work. It is knowing that in these times, we must activate our faith. We have God-given power in our tongues so when we speak life into a dead situation and trust God; it shall come to pass.

When storms come in our lives, it is very vital that we trust God during difficulties. When we give our problems to God, He is faithful to take us through the storm. Storms only make us stronger. They also help us to not worry so much about our problems and to trust God to see us through them. The thing I like about putting my trust in God is that He will help me to go through the storm with ease. God will not judge us; He will be a great support system as we go through the storms of life. I stay equipped and ready for the storm. * Proverbs 3:5-6.

(King James Version) "Trust in the Lord with all thine heart; and lean not unto your own understanding. In all thy ways acknowledge Him, and He Shall direct thy your path."

Chapter 2

Understanding God's Plan for You

Do you know God's will for you? Are you willing to follow His plan? It is especially important that we understand God's plan for our lives. The Bible says in Jeremiah that God knows the plans for our life. (Jeremiah 29:11). It is vital that if we do not understand God's plan, we should pray to God for a clear understanding.

You should know that God already has a plan predestined for you. Before we entered our mother's, womb God had the plan set up for us. We must not be afraid. We must set goals, step out on faith, and follow through. Understanding God's plan will not lead you wrong. You must stand firm on the Word of God and trust Him. This is a major part of understanding God's plan for you.

Understanding God's plan for you is submitting to God's will. Fasting and praying for direction and hearing from God will help you better understand the plan. Understanding the plan requires us to follow directions. We should also have a listening ear to hear what God wants us to do. God's plan for us will help us to cope with unbearable situations and times of trouble. Understanding God's plan helps us to fight a little harder when we face difficult times. His plans for us will never fail us. God has our plan already in place. It is important that we listen to God's voice for instructions. Sometimes when waiting on God, we tend to get a little impatient and we want God to move right away. God's plan sometimes requires us to patiently wait until God tells us to move. God will give us specific directions according to the plan He has for us.

God's plans allow us to have a divine connection to the King and the Kingdom. This connection can be strengthened through prayer. Fasting also strengthens the connection. It helps your health and relationship with Christ to become stronger; you must have the will to follow the plan God has for you. God's plan for you is uniquely designed for you. It is tailor-made. He has certain obstacle courses and challenges for you to face before you earn your reward.

There are some strategies you can use to discover God's plan for you. The Bible declares in 2 Timothy 2:15, "Study to show thyself approved unto God, a workman that needed not to be ashamed, rightly dividing the word of Truth." Another strategy is to seek God for directions on understanding the personal plan God has for you. Once you understand the plan, you can position yourself for greatness. When God is in it, there is no limit. God's plan for you will never allow you to fail, falter, or give up. The plan is designed to be motivation for you. Self-motivation is one of the best tools to use when trying to understand God's plan for you. Even when you fail it is important that you do not stay down but instead muster up enough strength to get back up again. It is during the times of failure that we really listen to the voice of God. This will help us to know where we went wrong and develop another plan of action to defeat the enemy and his tactics.

God's plan for you enables you to seek Him more because you are trying to understand what His plan entails for your life. God's plan will keep you on the straight and narrow but even when you fail, God's plan allows you to get back up and try again. This plan is designed to keep us afloat and a-breast through the Word of God. If there is something we do not understand about our God-given plan, it is then we can search the scriptures to see where we may have been in error. Then God allows us to use the scriptures to get it right so we can stay on the right path according to the plan.

Over the past few years, God has showed me different areas of the plan He has for me. I know that through the will of God, my earthly purpose is to inspire others. I know that God's plan must be fulfilled. I am thankful to God for making me in such a unique way that I can be a blessing to others. Being born with a disability, caused me to develop my own way to complete daily tasks and get the same result as those born without a disability.

God's plan for you may be a little difficult to accept at first, but you must trust God that He will never leave you nor forsake you. God's plan for your life is for you to learn valuable lessons, be prosperous, and bless others. The Master's plan will rearrange you, save you and change your life. God's plan will change your life and give you an amazing story, and He will also give you what He promised, eternal life.

God's plan for us will be a beacon of light when we face difficulties and feel that the weight of the world is on our shoulders. God uses His plans to see if He can trust us. When we face hardships, it is during these times that God's plan allows us to see how strong we really are.

God's plan for us is strategically designed to take certain types of problems head-on. The plan also prepares us for battle against the adversary when necessary. As Christians today, it is important that we work diligently to follow each component of God's plan for us. It is equally important that we ask God before we act on any part of His plan. It is vital that we get an understanding of all these things.

The plan God has for us is a golden roadmap to be a faithful Christian. The plan gives us step-by-step directions to ensure that we understand our personal plan. God does not create everyone is planning the same because just as He created everyone physically different, He created the plan spiritually different because everyone is not on the same spiritual level. It takes some of us longer than others to grow spiritually. God's plan allows us to be stronger through His strength. 1 John 4:4b. Greater is he that is in you, then he that is in the world."

Chapter 3

Facing Your Fear Through Grace

Has anyone ever told you that grace and mercy brought them through? When you face things you are frightened by, know that but you must call on God in these times. It is easier to face your fear when you have God on your side. Those twins called grace and mercy need to be in your emergency kit when fearful situations arise. The Bible declares that God's grace is sufficient for us. This applies even when we have fears.

Facing your fears can be both physically and emotionally challenging, but this is when you trust God even the more. Facing your fears head-on helps you to become a more willing vessel for God. There were several instances in my past when I had to face my fears; and had it not been for grace, I really don't know how I would have made it each year. When I started a new school year, I was always fearful because of how the other students would view me because I looked different from them. The way I was able to get over despair is that I explained to the other kids that although I am physically challenged due to my birth defect, I still can do the same things they do just in a different way.

Facing your fears through grace means depending on God to take your slingshot and rock and defeat your giants. The bigger they are, the harder they fall. When you have fears pressing you, it is then you lean and depend on God more. God's grace allows you to look your fears in the face and say, "I will face and conquer you." Though I go through the fire, I will not be defeated; I will win. Facing your fears through grace gives you strength to face challenges. Grace will cover all; the good, the bad, the ugly, and the in-between. It is because of grace that we can take on our own battles against the enemy.

I am thankful that through God's grace, He has helped me to overcome the fears I face daily. Without God, I know I cannot face the challenges and fears I have. I am strong enough to face the giant and take him down with my God-given strength. Sometimes when facing your fears, you may feel you have to stand alone; but through God's grace, you are never alone. There are some challenges when facing fears, but we must stand firm and trust God when the fears come upon us. Facing our fears helps us to cope with daily problems and develop strategies to solve them. Facing your fears can be difficult at times but when God is on your side, it makes things a whole lot easier.

When we face fears, we have victory over the enemy. We can stand firm and take on the problem like a champ. When we face our fears and take our problems to God, He will work it out. Defeating the enemy and facing your fears help you to obtain favor with the Lord. It is amazing how even in your fearful moments, you can gain strength to push forward.

Facing your fears helps you to become who God wants you to be. Sometimes we must go through things to beat the odds to prove that we are worthy. Facing your fears can also help you to follow your dreams. Once you block your fears out of the way, it makes reaching your goals and following your dreams easier. Although facing your fears can be rough, once it is done, you can move on and focus more on the victory you have obtained from the Lord.

When facing your fears, always know that God is with you. Do does not give up on victory; it is just around the corner. We must continue to look to God when we are faced with fears. I know from facing personal fears that God will never leave you; He is faithful to face your fears with you. * Matthew 28:20b "Lo, I am with you always, even until the end of the world. Amen."

Chapter 4

Finding Favor with God

Have you ever wondered why God blesses you in a way that is mind-blowing? God can bless you in a way that will bless your socks off. I have been blessed in so many ways. At first, it was scary until I was reassured that the favor of God was on my life. Finding favor with God is something that it is rewarding through our lifestyle and the character we portray in and outside of the walls of the church.

When you ask God to grant you favor, He will do it according to your works. When you are obedient to God's will, He will bless your life. Finding favor with God can be easy when you do your part. This may include studying the scriptures daily, praying more, and fasting. Fasting will assist you in finding favor with God. It teaches you the benefits of waiting on something from God. Waiting on God's favor can be greatly beneficial. While you are waiting, you can encourage others who may want to give up holding on and wait patiently on God. The favor of God can lead you to victory. Favor will take you higher in God and help you to understand that God really wants to bless you.

He will also allow you to know and understand that He has His hands on your life. When God has His hands on you, it is almost a promise that the blessings He has for you will be yours. Favor with God is so rewarding and helps you to strive hard to accomplish what you set out to do. Favor from God is simply granted through obedience. When you expect something from God, pray that He showers you with favor from above. It is important to understand that when you pray to God, He is listening to your every cry. Crying out to God is a way of surrender. Surrendering to God means committing to the way and will of God.

There are some wonderful blessings you can have when you give up the things of the world and pray for God's favor. These things can consist of a lavish lifestyle, substance abuse, compulsive gambling habits, and more that will hinder you from the blessings God has for you. God will take care of His own and having favor is an extra incentive. For example, when you work on your job and your supervisor explains the possibility of receiving a little bonus or gift of some sort, it is concerned as extra. This is also the same when you are doing Kingdom work. For instance, favor covers you so you will not be injured on the job. You know God has granted His favor when you are protected while working for Him. God's favor is truly a blessing sent from Heaven. The favor of God allows you to go through things you never thought you could. When you have God on your side, you will be surprised at the things you can accomplish. God's favor will give you strength during your weakest times. God's favor is like a warm embrace when you are at your lowest point.

If you have God's favor it is almost as if you have taken a good dose of medicine to help you get rid of an affliction. God knows just who to allow to go through every situation. God knows who is strong enough to handle what and who cannot handle certain trials. If you are blessed with the favor of God, you should be thankful. When you have favor, you should honor God with that by devoting more time to study the Word of God, fasting and praying. God assigns us people to work with and assist. This is beneficial in Kingdom-building.

As Christians, it is important that we are willing vessels and willing to build for the Kingdom. God has given us specific directions on how we can uplift the Kingdom and draw others to Christ. All we must do is lift the Kingdom and God will do the drawing. The Bible says in Job 12:32, "If I be lifted up, I will draw all men unto me." God has all power so all we must do is exalt the Lord and more people will come to Christ. We must thank God for the favor He has granted us. We look toward God for continued love and favor. If you are looking for God's favor, open up your heart and let Him in. * Philippians 4:13: "I can do all things through Christ which strengthens me."

Chapter 5

Our Words Have Power

Our words have power to defeat the enemy. It is important that we are careful what we allow to come out of our mouths. We should always guard our lips. Sometimes we say things that may hinder us from receiving blessings from God. We must be careful what we speak over our lives and the lives of others. Power in our words makes a stronger and we can face different situations without being fearful.

Having power in your words can allow you to speak over others and watch God's blessings be manifested in their lives. For instance, the Bible declares, in Mark 16:18, if we believe in our hearts, we can lay hands on the sick and they will recover. Power to lay hands on the sick is rewarding because it shows the effects of your effectual fervent prayer. Power in your words can help you to speak positive things into the lives of those who may be going through tough situations. For example, you may save someone's life. The person could be contemplating suicide and your words alone could be their saving grace. Your words can save their lives and give them the opportunity to be an advocate against suicide and speak blessings into the lives of others in the same type of situation.

Words have power to defeat the odds. As a child, I was determined that I would walk and after a lot of hard work, I did it. Because my words have power, I was able to accomplish what I set out to do. It is important to speak positive things into the atmosphere. Power in our words, enables us to stand firm, stick your chest out, and beat the odds. Power in our words is use as hope when we are going through, and it helps us to face challenges head-on.

Words are powerful to outweigh the good and bad. We can engage in situations where the power of God can help us to stand firm when it is time for battle. Power in our words where is helps us to claim the victory. Power encourages us that the devil is defeated. We serves him notice right now that he does not have power over us. It is through power we can give our problems to God, and He helps us to use the power within to speak to our problems. Power in your words gives you strength. It helps you to take on any problem and come up with a master plan to resolve it. There is purpose in going through sometimes which allows us to speak to the mountain and watch it move.

We have the power to speak to our enemies and they will fall like giants. I am grateful for the power God has given us. This God-given power has granted me the ability to face giants I never thought I could. I was able to take them down with the power God has blessed me with from above. * Proverbs 18:21: "The powers of life and death lies in the tongue."

Chapter 6

The Benefits of Prayer

Prayer a very essential part of life. It is beneficial and serves as a direct connection to God. How strong is your connection with God? Prayer strength is your connection. There are so many benefits to having a prayer life with God. The benefits of prayer help you to gain a clear understanding of the things God wants you to do.

The benefits of a prayer life help you to have a closer walk with Christ. It allows you to open your ears and your heart to be receptive to the will of God. Your benefits allow God to open doors that otherwise would be impossible. Having benefits from God through prayer gives us a direct way to petition the throne of grace. Jesus died on the cross and interceded on our behalf; this was great and beneficial to us. Since Jesus died on the cross, we no longer need man to go to God for us. Jesus tore the veil from top to bottom, which gives us a direct connection to God. Prayer stretches the connection so we can make our own petitions to God and having a strong prayer life makes your connection with God stronger and stronger.

The benefits of prayer help us to resist the devil and watch him flee. Prayer puts the devil on the run. Prayer will keep you sustained when the devil throws his fiery darts. Prayer is beneficial in an individual's life. Prayer helps you to gain strength and bounce back from tough situations. Prayer helps us to fight our battles and claim the victory through Jesus. Prayer gives us a line that is direct to Jesus. This gives us the opportunity to talk to Jesus without having to go through a middleman. Prayer is the simple gateway we go through to get to God. When we prays to God, we must trust and believe that He is going to grant us our requests.

The benefits of a prayer life help us not to be ashamed to ask God for our needs. It is a wonderful feeling when we pray to God and watch Him bless us. Watching our prayers be manifested is truly a blessing from God. Prayer is important because it helps us to get through basic problems as well as more tougher situations. Prayer helps us to understand that God will not leave us comfortless. When Jesus went to die for the sins of the world, He made it easier to pray because He left us a comforter.

Prayer helps us to have a direct line of communication with God. For example, we may be afraid to ask for certain things but because we have an effective prayer life, we are more confident in asking. Prayer helps us to fully understand our walk with Christ. Our relationship with God is just as significant as our relationship with our partner. Prayer gives us unlimited access to God. We can ask whatever we will in Jesus' name through prayer and supplication. This creates a direct connection to God the Father, the Son, and the Holy Spirit.

Prayer allows the Holy Trinity to work to make life-changing decisions that can affect our lives forever. Being faithful and praying daily has benefits that can change your life for years to come. When you devote time to prayer, God will reward you with wonderful benefits. Prayer is one of my God-given ways to petition the throne of grace and wait for answers. * James 5:16b: "The effectual fervent prayer of the righteous man avails much".

Chapter 7

Seek God with Your Whole Heart

The Bible declares, Psalms 63:1, "Early in the morning will I seek thee." It is important that we seek God with our whole heart. It is vital that we wait for instructions on seeking God. There are genuinely great rewards when seeking God. God will allow you to see things in a whole new light.

Seeking God allows you to be more transparent with others. Seeking God allows you to shine and give people the chance to see your life. The Bible tells us according to Matthew 15:15-16, "Let your light so shine, so men may see your good works and glorify our father which is in heaven. Seeking God with your whole heart helps to give God glory and honor. Do not be afraid to seek God because there are great rewards for seeking Him. For instance, seeking God allows you the opportunity to spend quality time with Christ, which is much needed. Seeking God can guide you but may get a little tired but know that in these times, you need to pray to God for strength and understanding. He will give you the peace that surpasses all understanding. You will not regret the personal time you spend seeking Him.

When you are determined to seek God, He will surely bless your life. Seeking God allows Him to bless those who are connected to you. Seeking God gives us divine connection with Him. It helps us to adapt to the will of God. It is very vital to seek God with your whole heart to gain direct instructions from Him on the plans He has for you. Seeking God helps us to choose to stay on the winning team with Christ. When you seek God, that makes Him the head of your life and you go over and beyond to please Him with your Christian walk. As a Christian, it is important to stay in the will of God.

Seeking God guarantees a stronger walk with Christ. When you seek God, open your eyes, ears, and heart so you can absorb the necessary information to enhance your will to seek Him wholeheartedly. It is very beneficial to seek God when times get tough. The tough times make you stronger and help you to believe more in yourself. Seeking God wholeheartedly will help you find yourself. It can also show you where God wants you to be spiritually. When seeking Him sincerely, He will reveal your God-given gifts and talents. * Matthew 6:33: "Seek ye first the kingdom of God, and his righteousness; and all these things shall be added unto you."

Chapter 8

Run on for God

God has a work that must be completed in each of us. We must not be afraid to run for Him. Running the race helps our blessings to be more effective as today's Christians. We cannot give up in the race. We must be fearless and run on and wait with a holy boldness. God gives us power not to be weary during the race.

Our God-given power is to bless others while we encourage them to run on and prepare for the great reward. Run on with God on your side. God will be your very present help in the time of trouble. The ability to run on gives you the chance to get instructions in the next thing God wants you to do. If you are willing to run, you can develop a master plan. It is essential to run on for Christ because with each stride it tells you exactly what to do to make this race a whole lot better.

When running this race, you cannot help but to look and see how you can be a positive impact on others. As Christians, it is our job and assignment to see how we can assist others we work with when preparing for the race. We are running for God; we face all types of obstacles and stumbling blocks. I am so thankful I chose to run for God; it is so rewarding. He will give us just what we need when we are prepared for the race. Preparation takes time and willingness to run, and we must remember to do it in Jesus' name. God will help us to run and if necessary, He is there to help us through every stride. Running time for Christ helps us to come up with a strategic plan to develop a way to meet others.

Running for Christ helps us to reach others and give them insight on what God expects from us. The race lets us know that giving up is never an option and we need to push harder and keep on running. There is truly a blessing when you know you are you ready for Christ. Your help and running allows others to see what God expects of us when He demands us to run for Him as a bold, willing Christian ready for battle. As important as it is to run on and be a blessing to others, we must also run on and bless the Kingdom of God. Have you ever imagined how running for God can influences your life as a Christian? We can be an example for others to follow when they get excited about running for Christ, and they can use our life as a roadmap. Your Christian walk can help you to build a healthier relationship with others who otherwise may not know Christ. Our life may be the only Bible that some people will read. This helps us to represent Christ and show others who side we are on. * Isaiah 40:31: "They that wait on the Lord shall renew their strength, they shall run and not be weary, they shall walk and not faint."

Chapter 9

How Deep Is Your Love for Christ?

This chapter was inspired by a man I heard minister in a youth revival. It is important that we have a special love for Christ. It must be different from any other kind of love. Our love for Christ should draw us closer and closer to Him. Christ loves us so much, and He is good this to love each other as I said. God told us to love others as he loves us

The love we have for Christ needs to show outside of the four walls of the church. If you live by the fruit of the Spirit, then you will gain a deeper love for Christ. This will also give you a stronger love for others. This alone is enough to bless God and give Him praise. God is awesome so we need to pray for a different relationship and a more genuine love for our God. Having a devoted relationship with God allows doors to either be open or closed. We must live and depend on Jesus by creating a deeper relationship with Him. This requires you to fast, pray, and devote time to helping others learn how to obtain a deeper relationship with God. Never doubt the relationship you have with Christ.

The Bible declares in 2 Corinthians 5:17, that if any man be in Christ, he is a new creature; old things are passed away and all things become new. We must be thankful for each new creation. Even when we think about who we are, we should be grateful. The relationship and deep love we should have for Jesus makes things that seem impossible to us, possible. *John 3:16: "For God so loved the world that he gave his only begotten son, that whosoever believeth in him should not perish, but have everlasting life."

Chapter 10

God Is in Control of the Storm

Most times, we believe God is in control of a situation when things are good. But on the other hand, when things go bad, we tend to put God on the back burner. Having faith does not exempt us from having problems. Difficult times make us wonder, God, where are you? He uses the storms and He allow others to go through to put us where we need to be. Your storms can blow you from A to B and place you in a position where God can use you.

God allows everything to happen with His permission. This means that sometimes you have to face the storm, not because you're doing something wrong but to make you better. Most times it is because you are doing something right that the devil attacks you, and God is right there to pull you through. When you are going through the storm, it gets you one step closer to your destiny. In some storms, we get discouraged; but your storm will not keep you from your destiny. God is in control and minor setbacks will not keep you from reaching your goal. When God is in control, wherever He takes you is where He wants you to be. Since God is in control of every storm, let the storms motivate and promote you. God knows how to shift your storm to an instant breakthrough. Going through the storm can be helpful because God wants to move the obstacle that show you his favor on your life. God is in complete control of the storm and he is so powerful that you never show evidence of the storm.

In the storm, God knows how to direct the wind so you can help others. God has your best interest at heart. Do not give up on your dreams; God is in control. It is important to be good to others when you are going through your storm. Storms are known as tests that will eventually become your testimony. Storms are sometimes considered as battles. Some things can only be learned or obtained in battle. Airplanes take off with the wind not against the wind, because of the control. The control God has allowed us to be as eagles. Going through the storm encourages us to trust God and not be afraid. We got through the storm to make us appreciate the sunshine. We can sing songs like, "The storm is almost gone. I can see the sun peeping through the clouds. The storm is almost gone." This song was written by gospel recording artist Dorothy Norwood.

Storms give us strength and prepare us for better. When we count on God, the storms we face become easier to go through. We are faced with storms that help us to grow in Christ. Do not give up on your God-given power when you go through the storm. * Proverbs 10:25: "When the storms of life come, the wicked our world away, but The Godly have a lasting Foundation."

Chapter 11

Have an Attitude of Gratitude

Having an attitude of gratitude is important and will help you to reach higher heights and deeper depths in Christ. When you have a relationship with God, your attitude goes through transformation. God is trying to let you know that you have a reason to praise Him. Let us have a spirit of gratitude; it can be beneficial to us. This will allow us to receive the blessings God has promised us. When you have an attitude of gratitude, you should stand in a posture of praise. God has blessed us with more than we are worthy of, so it is important that we commit our ways to God. your attitude can be beneficial you get the desires of your heart when God becomes the desires of your heart. Changing your attitude allows you to lay down what you want and commit to God's will.

We must trust God and He will allow your wildest dreams to come to pass. Your attitude will improve when you realize that your life is not falling apart but, He is putting you back together. Do not tell everybody what God told you to do. Move in silence and set goals to achieve your dreams. Improving your attitude requires studying the Word for yourself. Having an attitude of gratitude requires you to stop engaging in things that are not of God.

Your access to God is unlimited. You can call on Him when you are in need and He will answer you. It is important that you get to the point where God becomes the desire of your heart. We must see beyond the things we need. *Psalm 37:5 "Commit everything you do to the Lord, trust him, and he will help you."

Chapter 12

The Effects of the Secret Place

There are several effects of having a secret place. Everyone should have a secret place they can go to. It is our mission to guard our secret place. Do not let everything and everyone in your secret place. When your secret place is contaminated, it affects everything. Your secret place is hollowed and must be consecrated.

People who are in peace or not letting negativity take over. As Christians, we must protect our secret place; do not allow negativity to make you feel sorry. It is important not to let the devil harm your secret place. Serve an eviction notices to the things you do not want in your secret place. In your secret place, do not let the turmoil get on the inside. It is impossible to stop what goes on outside around your secret place, but you do have control of what goes on inside of it. The secret place allows you to protect your inner sanctuary. You cannot stop the storm from coming, but you can stop them from getting in your way. It is very vital that we honor God by doing the right things.

Let what God promised you give you inner peace. We must be careful of what and who we let get close to us. Keep your circle small. Do not let the small things keep you from reaching your full potential. Let go of things that can harm you. Keep your secret place covered in prayer and watch God bless your life. *Proverbs 4:23: "Guard your heart Above All Else, for it determines the course of your life."

Chapter 13

Rise Above Your Opposition

We can rise above opposition by taking the first step and that is stepping out on faith. There is a door wide open that may have adversities but we can pull through. The setback is a setup for a major comeback. The opposition shows that God is in control. Opposition is proving that promotions are coming. Because of opportunity there will be opposition. The giants you face were not sent to defeat you but to be an extra push and in turn increase the anointing on your life.

God is going to prove that you are anointed. People will see the favor of God on you. It is important that we do not run away from the giants but instead, run to one who defeated all giants at the cross, God. We will rise above opposition and the enemy is not going to defeat us, this fight is going to establish us. God will give you what you need; the level of influence will be amazing. Rising above your opposition will increase your insight and empower you in a way like never. This will be life changing. It makes it easier for God to use you for His Kingdom. You are designed by the greatest Designer of all times.

God is making you stronger, so do not complain about your giant. Instead, you should thank God for them; the giants make you fight harder and defeat them. It is especially important for us to stay in faith; do not be surprised when God blesses you and some people do not celebrate you. The celebration is for you and to prove to others did they have the same opportunity. When you are doing the right thing, God is getting ready to bless you. Sometimes you will have to walk away from things that will try to tempt you, but know you have the strength to do it. The important thing is that it is not where you have been, its where you're headed.

No one can stop your destiny. Do not argue with them because they are not that important. God opposes people who oppose you. When opposition comes, keep moving forward. Your time is too valuable to waste with people who do not really matter. Avoid some people opinion of you for the sake of peace. We must rise above opposition and watch God bless us; we should be the peacemaker.*Romans 12:2: "Do not be conformed to this world, but be ye transformed by the renewing of your mind, that by testing you may discern what is the will of God, what is good, acceptable, and perfect."

Chapter 14

God Will Provide

God will provide the needs of His children through grace and mercy. We have grace for whenever an attack comes our way. It is important to praise God through the attack. The attack might start at eye level but by the time it gets to you, it may be at foot level. Do not let things get in your way that will make you stop loving who you are. God will provide; He loves us through whatever we go through. God loves us through any problem we face.

God is the creator, sustainer, protector, provider, comforter, corrector, and father of all. God is about to create something new in our lives. God becomes the Creator in Genesis. God is about to create space for you and what you carry. God provides us with a sustainer in Acts 17:28, which states that in God, we live, move, and have our being possible. God provides us with the protector. If it were not for the protection of God, we would all be lost. God will provide for us when we are going through tough times. God is truly a provider. He will super-naturally provide for us. He is a good comforter and He comforts us when we are weary. God is the best corrector known to man; His love allows Him to be straightforward with us. He is a corrector and is willing to do what is necessary to get us back on track. He chastises those He loves.

God will discipline us when we need it. God the father is always good and His blessings prove just how good He is. God's blessing is favor on our life. Forgot to provide for us according to Matthew 11:28-29, we must rest in God and wait. God provides for us when we trust Him. In

Proverbs 3:5-6, He instructed us to, "Trust in the Lord with all thine heart, lean not to your own understanding, and all that ways acknowledge Him, and He Shall direct thy path. Just as we trust God to provide, we must obey His will and His Word.

We must trust God to do a new thing in us. God will provide everything that is needed for us to be successful. We must trust God and believe that He is going to do what He promised. It is important we believe that God can and will provide for us. In these times, you may think God have left you alone but you must know that God will provide in His own time. God Is providing for us daily even when we do not realize it. We are provided with food, clothes, and shelter so that we can live freely. We should be thankful to God for providing us with the necessities we need. Even though we do not deserve it, He blesses us repeatedly.* Philippians 4:19: "And my God shall supply every need according to his riches in glory by Christ Jesus."

Chapter 15

Blessings for Praying for Others

God blessings are a wonderful incentive when you pray for others. Praying for others gives you the opportunity to stand in the gap on their behalf. It helps you to create prayer warriors so when you are going through, you can count on someone else to pray for you. There are people God wants us to pray for to help be Kingdom Builders for God. We are to intercede on their behalf and lift them up.

Lifting people up in prayer is essential. When you pray for others, you are sowing a seed for God to help you and them. Job prayed for his friends and his health was restored. Press him to lighten up the load. When you pray sincerely for others, the angels begin to work. Prayers really make a difference in your life and in the lives of others. Praying for others is beneficial because it may be what they need just to keep them going.

Blessing from praying for others helps us to understand what we need to do in secret and God will reward us openly. Secret prayer causes the universe to make change happen that we could never imagine. Prayer makes the heavens stand still. The angels want to hear our prayers. It is then when God gives them instructions on what we need. Our prayers cause supernatural things to happen. Your prayer can help you overcome illnesses.

Do not be selfish when you pray. When you pray for yourself, pray for others and watch the boomerang effect. Prayer is powerful and helps others to find their potential. It is important to cover everyone and everything in prayer. Prayer is important because God is at work behind the scenes. Your faith and prayer life may cause someone to change their life for the better. Prayer helps people around us who are broken to pick up the pieces and move forward.

Prayer is more important than the family we come from, the degrees we have obtained, or the positions we currently hold. Prayer is a nice little too necessary for everyday living. Prayer gives us hope to follow our dreams. It is our way to connect to God. God wants us to encourage others. God has blessed us, so it is important to bless others. You did not get where you are on your own, so be grateful to God. When you pray for others, it is powerful, and you can watch the manifestation of God. Remember to take time to pray for others and God will bless you for your faithfulness. * Matthew 6:6: "But when you pray, go away by yourself, shut the door behind you, and pray to your father in private. Then your father, who sees everything, will reward you."

Chapter 16

The Importance of Staying in the Game

When you think about staying in the game, difficulties try to take you out. It is important to stay focused and keep an open mind. You may have a reason for feeling sorry, or have guilt, but you do not have a right to. It is important to shake of self-pity. You cannot let life's issues illness, divorce, and other things get in your way. Do not let this be an excuse for you to sit on the sidelines and watch. Sometimes you must play despite the pain from the battles that you have faced. I would rather be in the game in pain than, sitting on the sidelines watching. You must not let injuries allow you to sit on the sidelines when you are needed in the game. You must encourage yourself and say, I am hurting but I am here.

We must not let bad situations make us better. We must make up our minds to stay in the game. God still deserves praise despite what we go through. People who are hurting tend to hurt others who are hurting. Staying in the game requires sowing seeds. Trust and believe that God sees your seeds as effort. Another important point is to nurse your wounds while in the game. God has greater for those who stay faithful even when pain arises. If you move forward, God will take your scars and turn them into stars. Arise from the discouragement and, shake back, shake loose, and shake free; God has not forgotten about you.

God has a plan for your life. When one door closes, God will open another. It is important that we do our part so God will do the rest. Understand that your life is not over because you had a setback. When you play in the game, God breathes favor on you. God is not concerned about ow you perform; He is happy that you are in the game. God sees your effort. When you honor God when times are tough, your praise will give the enemy a nervous breakdown. Remember that despite the pain, the rest of your life will be the best of your life.

Ultimately, being Healed from Within, starts with you. There must be a willingness to want to allow God to help you heal from past hurt and scars that can haunt you for years to come. Healing begins from within. Sometimes it is necessary to allow God to perform heart surgery on you and adapt to change. This devotional was written in hopes to help someone to be open to change and avoid their lives to be affected by guilt and shame. God can heal you from the inside out and completely transform your life. Healing from within can be beneficial in kingdom building. Be changed, be renewed, and be Healed from Within!!!! Be Blessed.

About the Author

Trineka Yashika Anderson was born June 5, 1985, to the late Gwenderine Anderson and the late Samuel Scott Jr. Despite losing my mom at an early age, my older sisters and I were raised by some amazing grandparents. The opposition of being born with a disability has inspired me to help others. I have never been one to allow my disability to hinder her hopes and dreams. The challenges I have faced in life have inspired me to become an author I am compelled to believe that through my writing, I will be able to motivate others to find their God-given purpose. I am thankful for this opportunity, and it is my sincere prayer that you enjoy this devotional and be on the lookout for other books to come.

Notes

Notes

Notes

Notes

Notes

Made in the USA
Monee, IL
01 April 2021